HEBREWS

BOOKS OF FAITH SERIES
Learner Session Guide

Janet M. Corpus

HEBREWS
Learner Session Guide

Books of Faith Series
Book of Faith Adult Bible Studies

Copyright © 2010 Augsburg Fortress. All rights reserved. Except for brief quotations in critical articles or reviews, no part of this book may be reproduced in any manner without prior written permission from the publisher. For more information, visit: www.augsburgfortress.org/copyrights or write to: Permissions, Augsburg Fortress, Box 1209, Minneapolis, MN 55440-1209.

 Book of Faith is an initiative of the
Evangelical Lutheran Church in America
God's work. Our hands.

For more information about the Book of Faith initiative, go to www.bookoffaith.org.

Scripture quotations, unless otherwise marked, are from New Revised Standard Version Bible, copyright © 1989 Division of Christian Education of the National Council of Churches of Christ in the United States of America. Used by permission. All rights reserved.

Web site addresses are provided in this resource for your use. These listings do not represent an endorsement of the sites by Augsburg Fortress, nor do we vouch for their content for the life of this resource.

ISBN: 978-0-8066-9781-9
Writer: Janet M. Corpus
Cover and interior design: Spunk Design Machine, spkdm.com
Typesetting: PerfecType, Nashville, TN

The paper used in this publication meets the minimum requirements of American National Standard for Information Sciences—Permanence of Paper for Printed Library Materials, ANSI Z329.48-1984.

Manufactured in the U.S.A.
14 13 12 11 10 1 2 3 4 5 6 7 8 9 10

CONTENTS

1 Who Is Jesus? (Part 1) — 5
Hebrews 1:1-14

2 Who Is Jesus? (Part 2) — 11
Hebrews 2:5-18

3 What Did Jesus Do? — 17
Hebrews 4:14—5:10; 9:24—10:1; 10:10-18

4 What Is Faith? — 23
Hebrews 11:1-40

5 How Shall We Live? — 29
Hebrews 12:1-17; 13:1-19

6 What If Faith Fails? — 35
Hebrews 4:12-13; 5:11—6:12; 10:19-29

SESSION ONE

Hebrews 1:1-14

Learner Session Guide

Focus Statement
The person Jesus Christ, Son of God, is fully divine, God's very being. In Jesus, we see and know God.

Key Verse
He is the reflection of God's glory and the exact imprint of God's very being, and he sustains all things by his powerful word. When he had made purification for sins, he sat down at the right hand of the Majesty on high.
Hebrews 1:3

Who Is Jesus? (Part 1)

 Focus Image

The Ascension, Giotto di Bondone / Arena Chapel, Cappella degli Scrovegni, Padua. © SuperStock/SuperStock

Gather

Check-in
Take this time to connect or reconnect with the others in your group.

Pray
God of heaven and earth, before the foundation of the universe and the beginning of time you are the triune God: Author of creation, eternal Word of salvation, life-giving Spirit of wisdom. Guide us to all truth by your Spirit, that we may proclaim all that Christ has revealed and rejoice in the glory he shares with us. Glory and praise to you, Father, Son, and Holy Spirit, now and forever. Amen. (*Evangelical Lutheran Worship*, second option for prayer of the day for Trinity Sunday, p. 37)

Focus Activity
Quickly write down three words that describe God. Then take a few minutes to meditate on these words as descriptions of Jesus.

SESSION ONE

Notes

Open Scripture

Read Hebrews 1:1-14.

- What words stand out most to you?

- What questions do you have?

- What is your emotional reaction?

Join the Conversation

Historical Context

1. Hebrews, one of the latest books of the Bible, was written sometime between 60 and 100 C.E., approximately 30 to 70 years after Jesus' death. This means some in the original audience were probably second- or even third-generation followers of Jesus Christ.

- Imagine yourself in the original audience, raised in the Christian faith from childhood, and now perhaps taking your faith for granted or neglecting it. You may be facing a hostile environment and growing weary of being faithful.

- Make a list of things that might be distracting you, not only from the faith, but also from other important aspects of your life, such as time with family and friends, sleep, and your favorite renewing activities.

- Brainstorm a list of things you could do in this situation to help bring your life back into focus.

SESSION ONE

2. The conversation of which Hebrews is a part is a conversation *within* a community of Jewish Christians. The controversy is not between being Jewish and being Christian. It is *within* Jewish tradition about a new development in that tradition. And so, throughout Hebrews, the author compares God's revelation in Jesus Christ with what has gone before in God's Word spoken through prophets in Hebrew scriptures, temple practices, and ritual traditions. In Hebrews 1:5-14, for example, a series of psalms (Psalm 2:7; 104:4; 45:6-7; 102:25-27; and 110:1) refer to Christ.

- How do you suppose the original audience reacted to this use of Hebrew scriptures?
- How does this connection between Hebrew scriptures and Christ affect your reading of Hebrews 1:1-14?

Literary Context

1. Throughout the book of Hebrews, you will find the author making comparisons. Signals for the comparisons are words such as *new, superior, better, more, excellent,* and the conjunction *but*.

- Review Hebrews 1:1-14. Find and list the comparisons in the text. What points do these comparisons make?

2. One of the concerns of Hebrews is to describe fully the person of Jesus. The author worships Jesus as Lord, and wants the audience to share that conviction.

- List the words in Hebrews 1:1-14 that describe Jesus. How do these descriptions assert that Jesus is Lord?

Lutheran Context

1. One Lutheran principle for reading and interpreting the Bible is the question, "What shows forth Christ?" Martin Luther says the Bible is like the manger holding the Christ child. Everything in the Bible points us and leads us to Christ.

- What do you think about the idea that everything in the Bible draws us to Christ?
- How does Hebrews 1:1-14 point you or lead you to Christ?

2. Another Lutheran principle for reading and interpreting the Bible is "Scripture interprets Scripture." To gain a better understanding of challenging passages of Scripture, we can look at related texts.

- Read John 1:1-3; 1 Corinthians 8:6; and Colossians 1:15-20. How do these texts affect your understanding of Hebrews 1:1-14? List what each text says about the relationship between God and Jesus.

 Notes

SESSION ONE

 Notes

Devotional Context

1. Take a moment to get quiet and comfortable. Look at the Focus Image for this session. Close your eyes for a few moments and hold the image in your mind's eye. Then share with another person what you see in the painting. What do you notice first? What emotional response do you have to the painting?

2. Sing together the first verse of "All Hail the Power of Jesus' Name!" (*LBW* 328, 329; *ELW* 634). Then sing together "You Are Holy" (*ELW* 525). How do these songs tell you that Jesus is Lord of all?

Wrap-up

Be ready to look back over the work your group has done in this session.

Pray

Power of the eternal Father, help me. Wisdom of the Son, enlighten the eye of my understanding. Tender mercy of the Holy Spirit, unite my heart to yourself. Eternal God, restore health to the sick and life to the dead. Give us a voice, your own voice, to cry out to you for mercy for the world. You, light, give us light. You, wisdom, give us wisdom. You, supreme strength, strengthen us. Amen. ("A prayer of Catherine of Siena," *Evangelical Lutheran Worship*, p. 87)

Extending the Conversation

Homework

1. Read the next session's Bible text: Hebrews 2:5-18.

2. Use what you learned and experienced in this session in daily devotions this week. In daily prayer, give thanks for knowing God in Jesus. Sing or recite aloud one of the hymns included in the session. Repeating the song "You Are Holy" several times can be a meditation in itself. Each day write a one-sentence prayer to God about yourself and your faith.

SESSION ONE

3. We are surrounded by distractions from what is most important to us. A minor crisis or sense of urgency about secondary commitments can distract us from our primary commitments. An advertisement can pull us toward things, activities, or people who aren't really important to us. Ruffled feelings can distract us from focusing on what's at the heart of an interaction. Weariness or a short temper can distract us from kindness and understanding. At the start of the week, make a list of the three or four people, relationships, activities, attitudes, or needs that are the highest priorities for your life, especially for your life this week. As you go about your daily activities this week, note how you are distracted. Being aware of distractions is part of learning to affirm and focus on what's most important.

Enrichment

1. If you want to read through the entire book of Hebrews during this unit, read the following sections this week.
Day 1: Hebrews 1:1-4
Day 2: Hebrews 1:5-14
Day 3: Hebrews 2:1-4
Day 4: Hebrews 2:5-9
Day 5: Hebrews 2:10-13
Day 6: Hebrews 2:14-18
Day 7: Hebrews 3:1-6

2. Many artists—painters, sculptors, composers, and others—have tried to convey Jesus' divinity. Search out and explore some of these on the Web or at your local library.

3. The Bible tells us that humanity is created in God's image (Genesis 1:26). Make a list of the descriptions of Jesus' divinity or highlight the descriptions in your Bible. They tell us something about God, in whose image we are created. What do these descriptions tell us about who we are? What do these descriptions tell us about others?

Notes

SESSION ONE

For Further Reading

A History of God: The 4,000-Year Quest of Judaism, Christianity and Islam by Karen Armstrong (New York: Ballantine, 1994).

Available at augsburgfortress.org:

Hebrews for Everyone by N. T. Wright (Louisville, KY: Westminster John Knox, 2004).

SESSION TWO

Hebrews 2:5-18

Learner Session Guide

Focus Statement
The person Jesus Christ is fully human, in every way like us. In Jesus we see and know God. In Jesus we see and know who God created us to be.

Key Verse
Therefore he had to become like his brothers and sisters in every respect, so that he might be a merciful and faithful high priest in the service of God, to make a sacrifice of atonement for the sins of the people.
Hebrews 2:17

Who Is Jesus? (Part 2)

 Focus Image

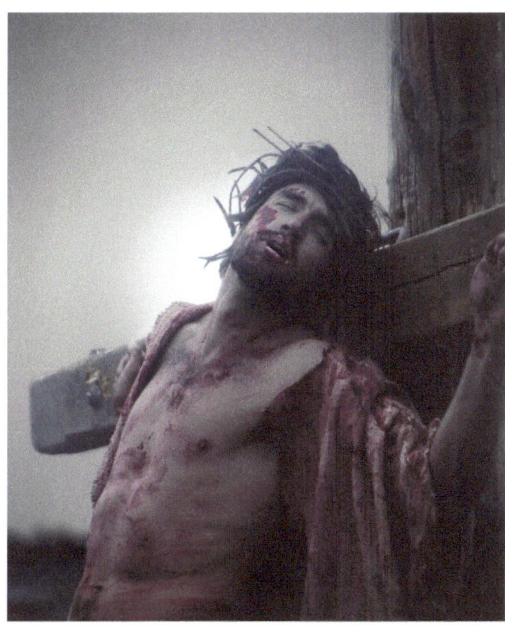

© Design Pics/SuperStock

Gather

Check-in
Take this time to connect or reconnect with the others in your group. Be ready to share new thoughts or insights about your last session.

Pray
Almighty God, you gave us your only Son to take on our human nature and to illumine the world with your light. By your grace adopt us as your children and enlighten us with your Spirit, through Jesus Christ, our Redeemer and Lord, who lives and reigns with you and the Holy Spirit, one God, now and forever. Amen. (Nativity of Our Lord III, *ELW*, p. 20)

Focus Activity
Take a moment to focus on Jesus as fully human. Stand or sit. Close your eyes. Focus on your posture—the angle of your head, the positions of your arms and legs, the shape of your back. Imagine that you are Jesus. Adjust your body as you imagine what it felt like to be him. What does it feel like? How is this different from your usual stance or posture?

SESSION TWO

 **Notes**

Open Scripture

Read Hebrews 2:5-18.

- How do you feel as you hear this passage?

- What word or phrase in the text grabs your attention most?

- What questions does the text raise for you?

Join the Conversation

Historical Context

1. Hebrews expresses the belief that God was flesh and blood in Jesus. This belief, called the *incarnation*, burst the confines of both Greek philosophical thought and Hebrew tradition.

- Read together the Nicene Creed. Look closely at the Second Article, the portion about Jesus. How does it talk about Jesus' humanity? What is the relationship between Jesus' humanity and Jesus' divinity in this creed?

- Look also at the Apostles' Creed, a shorter creed from an earlier time in the church. List differences and similarities in how this creed and the Nicene Creed teach the relationship between Jesus' divinity and humanity.

Literary Context

1. While Hebrews 1 emphasizes Jesus as divine, Hebrews 2 emphasizes Jesus as human.

- Read Hebrews 2:5-18 and underline or highlight the words and phrases that distinguish Jesus as human.

2. Jesus is described as the "pioneer" of salvation (Hebrews 2:10) and later as the "pioneer" of our faith (Hebrews 12:2). Pioneers may lead the way or break new ground in fields such as science, technology, music, or dance. Some pioneers are explorers—on earth or in space. Some pioneers are the "first," for example, the first female major league baseball umpire.

- Draw or describe what the word *pioneer* means to you. What does a pioneer do? Where does a pioneer go? What are followers' relationships to a pioneer? What kind of person does it take to be a pioneer?
- What does the image of a pioneer tell us about Jesus?

Lutheran Context

1. Lutheran theology includes several *paradoxes*—statements or realities that seem to contradict themselves. (For example, Martin Luther talked about Scripture as both law and gospel, and Christians as both saints and sinners.) The session Scripture text also contains paradoxes: Jesus is fully human and fully divine, and he is exalted because he becomes human and suffers and dies on the cross. As Luther writes, "[God] exalted Christ above all things when He cast Him down below all things" (Lectures on Hebrews, *Luther's Works* 29:127).

- How does the paradox of Jesus' full humanity and divinity help you and your faith?
- List the questions this paradox raises for you.

2. For Luther, becoming a parent brought with it faith lessons. In his children, Luther realized what it meant that God was born among us in Jesus Christ, an infant child.

- Identify ways in which human infants are vulnerable and dependent.
- How does it feel to imagine God as a human infant?

SESSION TWO

 **Notes**

Devotional Context

1. Sing together "Word of God, Come Down on Earth" (*ELW* 510). Then, as someone reads the words aloud slowly and deliberately, stand when the hymn refers to Jesus' humanity and sit when it refers to Jesus' divinity.

2. Sometimes people think of Jesus as somehow superhuman. Rather, Jesus is *fully* human. In Jesus, we see what God intends for human beings. Jesus is fully human and, in our human sinfulness, we fall short of being fully human. Write in a journal or make a picture of ways in which you feel or sense this in your life, and ways in which Jesus shows what it means to be fully human.

3. Turn your attention to the session's Focus Image. Imagine yourself as part of the scene. Describe what you experience and the emotions this evokes.

Wrap-up

Be ready to look back over the work your group has done in this session.

Pray

Brother Jesus, you are like me. Does that mean I am like you? In the week ahead, help me to follow your lead. And, in the week ahead, strengthen me in the face of challenges, that I may meet them with love and without fear, because I am confident in your love. Amen.

Extending the Conversation

Homework

1. Read the next session's Bible text: Hebrews 4:14—5:10; 9:24—10:1; 10:10-18.

2. Created in God's image, you have a body! This week celebrate your body—the fact that you are incarnate! Exercise as you are able—flex your feet and ankles right now, go for a walk this week, stretch your arms and legs as you are sitting. Make physical contact with people who are important to you and, as you do, thank God you are human. Eat responsibly. Take deep breaths. As you perform life's daily bodily care and preparations, celebrate these basic human realities as part of who God made you to be.

SESSION TWO

3. As you hear news of human suffering, pray for the people involved and their care and healing. Pray for peace. If you are able, do something to help alleviate suffering. Perhaps you can make a contribution of money. Perhaps you will write a letter to encourage legislative action. You may very well meet human suffering face-to-face in this week and have an opportunity to be of help more directly. When you see suffering, remember that Jesus is there.

Enrichment

1. If you want to read through the entire book of Hebrews during this unit, read the following sections this week.
Day 1: Hebrews 3:7-19
Day 2: Hebrews 4:1-11
Day 3: Hebrews 4:12-13
Day 4: Hebrews 4:14-16
Day 5: Hebrews 5:1-6
Day 6: Hebrews 5:7-14
Day 7: Hebrews 6:1-12

2. Do a Web search to learn more about the Arian controversy. For example, the First Ecumenical Council was called by the Roman emperor Constantine. What business did an emperor have convening a Christian assembly?

3. *The Green Mile* (Castle Rock Entertainment, 1999) is a film based on a Stephen King serial novel (Signet, 1996) of the same title. The story takes place on death row. The characters are guards and inmates, one of whom has special powers. That character, John Coffey, convicted of a heinous crime of which he is innocent, is both intimidating and childlike. *The Green Mile* is a story of how people respond in the face of human and divine powers at work in their midst, a story of great cruelty and great healing. Watch the film with others or, if you participate in a book group, suggest reading the novel.

 **Notes**

SESSION TWO

Notes

For Further Reading

And the Word Became History by Medardo Ernesto Gómez (Minneapolis: Augsburg, 1992).

The Gospel According to Jesus Christ by José Saramago (San Diego: Harvest Books, 1994).

SESSION THREE

Hebrews 4:14—5:10; 9:24—10:1; 10:10-18

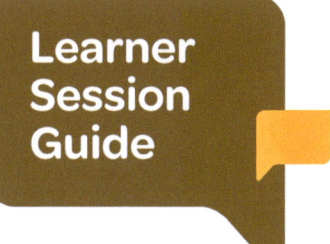

Learner Session Guide

Focus Statement
Because of who Jesus is—human and divine—Jesus is priest in both earth and heaven, in history and for eternity. By his obedience to God's work, Jesus perfected faith and fulfilled God's plan for our salvation.

Key Verse
Since, then, we have a great high priest who has passed through the heavens, Jesus, the Son of God, let us hold fast to our confession. For we do not have a high priest who is unable to sympathize with our weaknesses, but we have one who in every respect has been tested as we are, yet without sin. Hebrews 4:14-15

What Did Jesus Do?

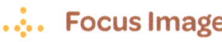 Focus Image

© BilderLounge / SuperStock

Gather

Check-in
Take this time to connect or reconnect with the others in your group. Be ready to share new thoughts or insights about your last session.

Pray
Lord Jesus, we gather here today because of you, who have called us together to study your Word. Open our hearts and minds, our eyes and ears to new understanding of who you are and of what you have done for the whole world, including us, each and every one. Amen.

Focus Activity
As a group, brainstorm a list of descriptive words and titles for Jesus.

SESSION THREE

 **Notes**

Open Scripture

Read Hebrews 4:14—5:10; 9:24—10:1, 10:10-18.

- What word, phrases, or images stand out to you?

- What questions do you have?

- What, if anything, is confusing or troubling?

Join the Conversation

Historical Context

1. In biblical times, the temple in Jerusalem was the center of Jewish faith. Within the temple, the "Holy of Holies" was seen as the place of God's presence. Only the high priest entered the Holy of Holies and only once a year.
   - Compare the layout of the temple (see the diagram below) with the layout of your congregation's worship space, noting the similarities and differences. What questions does this comparison raise?

2. In Jewish faith and tradition, the primary role of priests was to serve God. Priests were intermediaries, who spoke to God on behalf of the people and to the people on behalf of God. Some, notably the high priest, served God at the community's primary site of worship (the Jerusalem temple, while it was standing). The high priest played a particularly important role in the community's annual rite of sacrifice and renewal. This rite brought *atonement*—the restoration of the broken relationship between God and sinful humans. On the Day of Atonement, the priest entered the Holy of Holies and made sacrifices to atone for his own sins and the sins of all the people.

SESSION THREE

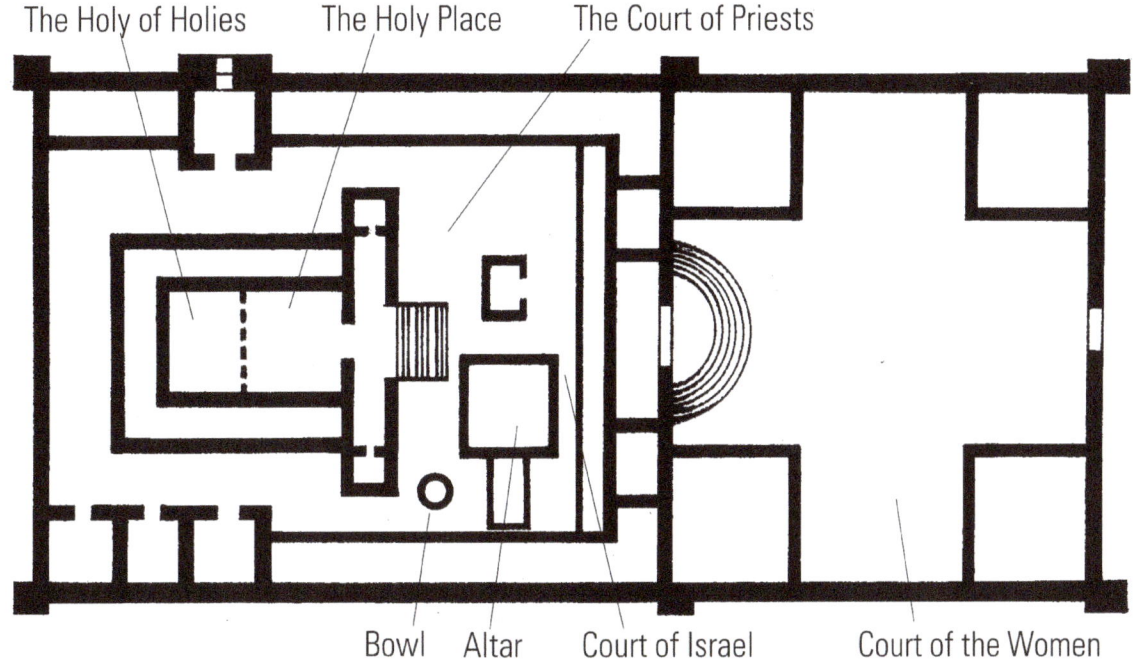

The Interior of the Temple in Jerusalem, New Testament Times. © 2009 Augsburg Fortress

- The Day of Atonement or, in Hebrew, Yom Kippur, is described in Leviticus 16–17. Scan these chapters and summarize the work of the high priest Aaron.
- Scan Hebrews 4:14—5:10; 9:24—10:1; and 10:10-18, and summarize the work of the high priests.

Literary Context

1. Christology is the area in theology that studies the person and work of Jesus Christ. It is also a major theme in Hebrews.

- Find out what Hebrews says about the person and work of Jesus Christ by scanning Hebrews 4:14—5:10; 9:24—10:1; and 10:10-18. List the comparisons made of Jesus to other priests, of Jesus' work to the work of others, and of Jesus' sacrifice to other sacrifices.
- Summarize what these comparisons say about the person and work of Jesus Christ. What did Jesus do in a physical sense? What did Jesus do in himself? What did Jesus do on earth? What did Jesus do in heaven?

Notes

SESSION THREE

 Notes

2. Hebrews likens Jesus to the Old Testament figure Melchizedek, who is only referred to twice outside Hebrews.
- Read Genesis 14:17-20; Psalm 110:4; and Hebrews 7, and list the similarities and differences between Jesus and Melchizedek.
- What do these comparisons say about the person and work of Jesus Christ?

Lutheran Context

1. Lutherans focus on God's actions, rather than our own. Martin Luther writes that Jesus "makes useless absolutely all the righteousness and deeds of penitence. . . . Before we repent, our sins have already been forgiven" (Lectures on Hebrews, *Luther's Works* 29:112).
- How do you react to Luther's statement? List the feelings and questions it raises for you.
- Review the session Scripture texts. How do they support Luther's statement?

2. In Hebrews' terms, as high priest, Jesus made atonement for all our sins once and for all. For Luther, this is the heart of the gospel, that our sins are forgiven. Jesus accomplished this work on the cross, when he said, "It is finished" (John 19:30). On the cross Jesus offered himself for our sake—and was exalted.
- Luther emphasized the importance of believing not only that Jesus did this work for us, but that Jesus did this work for you. Salvation is *for you*.
- Reflect on the Focus Image and on Jesus' work as high priest and as complete sacrifice. Then describe in words or drawings what Jesus did for you and how you feel about this.

Devotional Context

1. Hebrews uses the image of Jesus as Great High Priest. Make a list of ways you picture Jesus. Do you include high priest on your list? Why or why not?

2. Hebrews 4:16 says, "Approach the throne of grace with boldness." Be bold in your prayers to God. Take time for silence to consider things you may want to say, but feel aren't quite appropriate for prayer. For example, if there's something you're embarrassed to be thankful for, thank God for that thing. If you're angry with God about something, let God know it. If you are hiding something (even from yourself a bit), tell it. If you just don't understand something, ask for an explanation.

SESSION THREE

3. In Jesus Christ, we know God in flesh. In Jesus' work of salvation, he gave us direct access to God. Close your eyes and visualize a time or place where you experienced God's presence. Meditate on that experience. Savor it. Let yourself rest in it.

Pray

Pray or sing together "Now Thank We All Our God" (*LBW* 533, 534; *ELW* 839, 840).

Extending the Conversation

Homework

1. Read the next session's Bible text: Hebrews 11:1-40.

2. Attend worship with other members of your study group. Be mindful that we come to Holy Communion not to accomplish anything, but to receive and celebrate what has already been accomplished for us by God's grace—the forgiveness of all our sins in Jesus Christ. Following worship, take some time together to reflect on the experience.

3. Philippians 2:5-11 is an ancient confessional hymn about the person and work of Jesus Christ. Slowly read the words of this text aloud each day, taking time to hear the words as you speak them.

4. You have explored the work of Jesus Christ—and what Jesus has done for you. How would you describe that to someone else? Practice sharing what you would say about this to someone in your "comfort zone"—a member of your study group, church, family, or a friend. When opportunities arise, consider sharing within and beyond your normal comfort zone.

Enrichment

1. If you want to read through the entire book of Hebrews during this unit, read the following sections this week.
Day 1: Hebrews 6:13-20
Day 2: Hebrews 7:1-10
Day 3: Hebrews 7:11-19
Day 4: Hebrews 7:20-28
Day 5: Hebrews 8:1-7
Day 6: Hebrews 8:8-13
Day 7: Hebrews 9:1-10

2. As a group, invite a rabbi to meet with you to talk about contemporary Yom Kippur observance, as well as other traditions referred to in Hebrews. If your pastor and the rabbi are willing, ask them to talk with your group about Jewish-Christian relations.

 Notes

SESSION THREE

Notes

3. As a group or individually with a friend or acquaintance, attend a synagogue service. Take time following the service to debrief with one another and your host. How does the service compare to worship services you're used to? What surprised you? If portions of the service are in Hebrew, what was that like for you?

4. The Jerusalem temple has an important history, some of which is reflected in the Gospels. Particularly if you're a history buff, an architect, or interested in archaeology, you'll find it interesting. You can start with what the Bible has to say about the temple—from its architectural specifications to its use and abuse. From there, go online to see drawings of what the temple—really a series of structures—may have been like and to learn about its intriguing religious, theological, cultural, and political history.

For Further Reading

Available from augsburgfortress.org:

Fortress Introduction to Salvation and the Cross by **David A. Brondos** (Minneapolis: Fortress Press, 2007).

Holy Things: A Liturgical Theology by Gordon Lathrop (Minneapolis: Fortress Press, 1998). See especially chapter 6, "The Christian Sacrifice," pp. 139–58.

SESSION FOUR

Hebrews 11:1-40

Learner Session Guide

Focus Statement

Faith is hearing God's word with our whole lives—obeying God's promises in hopeful and expectant trust, despite appearances. The countless people who have gone before us and lived by faith are models and inspiration for us.

Key Verse

Now faith is the assurance of things hoped for, the conviction of things not seen. Indeed, by faith our ancestors received approval. By faith we understand that the worlds were prepared by the word of God, so that what is seen was made from things that are not visible. Hebrews 11:1-3

What Is Faith?

 Focus Image

© Design Pics / SuperStock

Gather

Check-in

Take this time to connect or reconnect with the others in your group. Be ready to share new thoughts or insights about your last session.

Pray

Draw your church together, O God, into one great company of disciples, together following our teacher Jesus Christ into every walk of life, together serving in Christ's mission to the world, and together witnessing to your love wherever you will send us; for the sake of Jesus Christ our Lord. Amen. (*ELW*, p. 75)

Focus Activity

Get comfortable. Close your eyes and recall someone you would describe as a person of faith. What is it about the person that makes that description appropriate? What feelings do you have about the person? Describe this person's life, relationships, and speech. What do you recognize as faith?

SESSION FOUR

Notes

Open Scripture

Read Hebrews 11:1-40.

- What in the text touched you?

- What images stood out for you?

- What surprised you?

Join the Conversation

Historical Context

1. God has provided many other exemplars of faith throughout history. For the original readers of Hebrews, in a Jewish community of the first century, the list of people in Hebrews 11 would have constituted a "roll call" of the faithful.

- What names are on your "roll call" of faithful people? Share the names and stories of some who are important to you. (They may be widely known; they may be known only to you.) How does sharing these names and stories affect you? Place the names on a timeline, according to the approximate dates of when each person lived.

- List the names of people included in Hebrews 11. How do you suppose the original readers of Hebrews were affected by this list of names?

SESSION FOUR

2. The faithful people listed in Hebrews 11 obeyed God's promises in hopeful and expectant trust, despite appearances.

- Form two groups, one to read about Noah in Genesis 6:13-14, 17-19, and the other to read about Abraham in Genesis 12:1-3 and 15:1-6. Report back to the large group on these questions: What did God ask this person to do? What did God promise? Putting yourself in Noah's or Abraham's position, how would you feel about God's proposition to you? What would you take into consideration before agreeing to what God asked of you? Would you do it? Why or why not?

Literary Context

1. The Greek word *hypostasis*, translated as "assurance" in Hebrews 11:1, also appears in Hebrews 1:3 and 3:14. In those places, it is translated as "very being" and as "confidence" (NRSV). It has also been translated as "substance" (King James Version and New English Bible) and "reality" (Harold W. Attridge, *Hebrews*, Hermeneia [Minneapolis: Fortress Press, 1989], p. 307). It is the same word used in the Nicene Creed to say that Jesus is "of one *being* with the Father."

- How does this affect your reading of Hebrews 11:1-3? Read that passage again, and then put it in your own words.

2. Reflect on the Focus Image for a few moments. Then, in a group of three or four, come up with a way to tell people today what faith is. Feel free to use a description, a simile (faith is like . . .), a story, a drawing, a pantomime, or some other medium.

Lutheran Context

1. Martin Luther writes, "Faith is God's work in us, that changes us and gives new birth from God. . . . It . . . makes us completely different people. It changes our hearts, our spirits, our thoughts and all our powers. It brings the Holy Spirit with it" ("Martin Luther's Definition of Faith: An excerpt from 'An Introduction to St. Paul's Letter to the Romans,'" tr. Robert E. Smith, Project Wittenberg, 1994).

- Read the quotation two more times. First, read it and list the *subjective* changes—changes we can feel or sense. Second, read the quotation and list the *objective* changes—changes that are real apart from what we might feel or sense. What difference do these two readings make in your image of what faith is?

2. Luther was emphatic that faith must precede good works. Works that proceed from faith are righteous. They rely on Christ's righteousness alone, Christ having perfected faith and sanctified believers. Works that precede faith rely on the person performing them. However good the works may be, they are a judgment on the person, who acts on his or her own righteousness, which cannot make the work itself or the person complete.

Notes

SESSION FOUR

 Notes

- What do you think about this? How would you describe the connection between faith and good works?

Devotional Context

1. Explore the nature of your faith. First, list three to five words that would be part of a description of your faith. Second, close your eyes and visualize your faith—what does your faith look like? Third, think of one reason why faith is important. Fourth, if you can, think of a piece of music—a hymn, a song, an instrumental tune, etc.—that somehow embodies what your faith is like. Finally, assume a pose that might convey your faith to someone looking at you.

2. Grounded in and responding to God's promise, faith has an inherent orientation toward the future. Looking back on the history of God's promises and on God's actions, faith anticipates God's own faithfulness in fulfilling promises and continuing to be God. The future is not without surprises. Yet, we know what the future is like: justice, peace, and freedom; all people eating together; all creation reconciled and made whole. We know this future from the past. We know this future in God's Word, which is God's promise. We know this future in Jesus Christ—Jesus' life, suffering, death, and resurrection.

- Imagine the future. First, consider Abraham and Sarah and the future in which they trusted: a promised land, a heavenly country, a child born in their old age. Consider their wandering in unknown territory, not knowing where they were going, much less the way there. They met obstacles as well as opportunities.
- Now, in your mind's eye or on paper, envision your future—the promises of God fulfilled for you. What does it look like?

Wrap-up

Be ready to look back over the work your group has done in this session.

Pray

Thank you for all those who, through the ages and in my own life, have witnessed to your love and faithfulness, to your justice and mercy. Make us such witnesses that our faith might help others to know your lovingkindness and faithfulness to all people and all creation. As we go about our lives in the coming days, let the light of our faith shine before others that they may see how we live and glorify you. Amen.

SESSION FOUR

Extending the Conversation

Homework

1. Read the next session's Bible text: Hebrews 12:1-17; 13:1-19.

2. This week as you go about your daily life, be mindful of the people you encounter whose faith examples are important to you. Take a moment to pray a word of thanks for them. If you are able and comfortable doing it, let these people know about your gratitude for their faith. As you express your thanks in person or in a note, give a concrete example of what you mean.

3. Faith grows by passing it on. It grows by contagion and it grows in the person who passes it on. Tell the story of someone whose faith has been an example to you. (If you would prefer, try writing or recording the story.) Tell a little about the person, the person's faith, and how it has affected you. If you are a parent, you might tell your child. You might tell another member of your family or a friend. Perhaps you might tell a coworker or neighbor. Surprisingly, you might find yourself telling the story in a conversation with a virtual stranger.

Enrichment

1. If you want to read through the entire book of Hebrews during this unit, read the following sections this week.
Day 1: Hebrews 9:11-14
Day 2: Hebrews 9:15-22
Day 3: Hebrews 9:23-28
Day 4: Hebrews 10:1-10
Day 5: Hebrews 10:11-18
Day 6: Hebrews 10:19-25
Day 7: Hebrews 10:26-39

2. Daily life carries images for our faith. What are your regular activities? Focus on one—cooking, typing, driving, teaching, running, filing, caring for a parent or child, cutting hair, knitting, wiring houses, waiting tables, preparing legal briefs, playing basketball. What are the individual actions that make up the whole? Is there an action that you can see as an image related to faith? For example, wait staff serve others, electricians provide light and energy for people's lives, office workers create order amid chaos. Begin with that single connection and gradually reflect on the entire activity, making other connections to faith.

 Notes

SESSION FOUR

3. Organize a faith-focused reading group. Particularly if people are busy, try using *A Celestial Omnibus: Short Fiction on Faith*, ed. J. P. Maney and Tom Hazuka (Boston: Beacon Press, 1998).

For Further Reading

Dynamics of Faith by Paul Tillich (New York: HarperOne, 2001).

Murder in the Cathedral by T. S. Eliot (New York: Harcourt Brace, 1963).

SESSION FIVE

Hebrews 12:1-17; 13:1-19

Learner Session Guide

Focus Statement

Jesus has perfected our faith. We can lay aside sin, which no longer binds us, and follow where Jesus has pioneered the way. Faith practices, like athletic practice, are part of how we condition ourselves for lives of following.

Key Verse

Therefore, since we are surrounded by so great a cloud of witnesses, let us also lay aside every weight and the sin that clings so closely, and let us run with perseverance the race that is set before us, looking to Jesus the pioneer and perfecter of our faith.
Hebrews 12:1-2a

How Shall We Live?

 **Focus Image**

© OJO Images / SuperStock

Gather

Check-in

Take this time to connect or reconnect with the others in your group. Be ready to share new thoughts or insights about your last session.

Pray

Gracious and loving God, we gather to be with you in your Word and with one another in you. Help us together to learn a way of life that not only sustains us in faith, but also witnesses to the great power of your love. As we gather here and always, keep us mindful of those who have not heard of your love, that we might learn boldness to proclaim in deed and word. Amen.

Focus Activity

Close your eyes and get comfortable. Imagine that you are on a path. A 500-pound (225 km) block is in your way. Try to move it. How does that feel? How does this affect your body? How does this affect your attitude? Slowly change your focus from the block to the path ahead. Jesus is walking toward you. When Jesus reaches the block, he picks it up and hurls it out of sight. He proceeds along the path, gesturing for you to come along.

Session 5: Hebrews 12:1-17; 13:1-19   29

SESSION FIVE

 **Notes**

Open Scripture

Read Hebrews 12:1-17; 13:1-19.

- In a word or phrase, what is your first reaction to these texts?

- What images stand out?

- What questions do you have?

Join the Conversation

Historical Context

1. The church has known persecution throughout its history. After Jesus' torture and execution, Jesus' followers were subject to the same threat. The book of Acts tells of persecution including arrests, beatings, imprisonment, and stoning. Some religious persecution was carried out within the Jewish community in the struggle over the new "Jesus movement," viewed by some as heretical. The Roman Empire, however, had the might and resources to be the primary source of persecution, beginning under Nero.

- Review Hebrews 12:1-17 and 13:1-19, and list words or phrases indicating that the original readers of Hebrews may have experienced persecution for their faith.

2. Imagine yourself as one of the original readers of Hebrews. Sometime in the past, you and your faith community, and perhaps family members, were persecuted for your faith. Either your faith was active enough that you were a threat, or perhaps you or those

SESSION FIVE

you knew were treated as an example to put fear in believers. Make some notes about how you feel. Discuss how persecution might have affected your faith and the practice of your faith.

- The persecution of Jesus' followers subsides over time. The memories of persecution remain, but you and those you know are safer now. How does this feel? Discuss how this turn of events might affect your faith and the practice of your faith.

Literary Context

1. In Hebrews 12:1-13, the writer uses imagery from an athletic contest to encourage readers to follow Jesus in faith.

- Scan Hebrews 12:1-13 and list words or phrases that refer to an athlete or athletic competition.
- Reflect on the Focus Image. In the "race" of faith, what does the "cloud of witnesses" do? What does Jesus do? What do we do?

2. Hebrews 12:12-13 says, "Lift your drooping hands and strengthen your weak knees, and make straight paths for your feet." To understand this image more fully, intentionally distort something about your posture. For example, let your hands droop, slouch, raise your shoulders to your ears (or put an ear to your shoulder), stand on one leg, or stick one hip out to the side. What does the rest of your body do in response? How do you compensate?

- Now return to your normal sitting or standing position. How does this feel? What does it do for your sense of self?

3. Portions of the session Scripture texts provide "instructions" for living as a follower of Jesus.

- Read Hebrews 12:14-16 and 13:1-17, listing the instructions provided in these passages. Which ones seem most important? Which seem easier to do than others? Which, if any, are confusing or troubling? Are there any instructions that surprise you?

Lutheran Context

1. The primary lens through which Lutherans read Scripture is that of law and gospel. God's law is everything God asks of us. Because we cannot do all that God asks, we must look to God for grace, mercy, love, and forgiveness. The gospel is everything God does for us.

- Review the session Scripture texts. Underline words or phrases that you hear as law, and circle words or phrases that you hear as gospel. What effect does doing this have on you?

 Notes

SESSION FIVE

 Notes

2. Hebrews 12–13 talks about how we should live. Yet we know that as sinners we are unable to do everything that God asks. No matter what we do, we cannot get everything right in our lives. What should we do, then, when we're uncertain about how to proceed, or must choose from options that all have problems or drawbacks? In a letter to his friend Philip Melanchthon, Martin Luther writes, "Be a sinner and sin boldly, but believe and rejoice in Christ even more boldly, for he is victorious over sin, death, and the world" (*Luther's Works* 48:282).

- What do you think Luther means by this advice? Tell about a time when you or someone you know acted or moved forward boldly in faith.
- Consider a dilemma you're facing. Describe or doodle your dilemma on a piece of paper. In what you've written or drawn, where is the focus of the unresolved issue? On that place, write the words, "I rejoice in Jesus Christ."

Devotional Context

1. Faith practices are actions that nurture the growth of faith. They are for every day, every moment, every place in our lives. Take a look at the ELCA's Faith Practices Wheel (on the next page). Several faith practices appear in the center ring, with related ministry areas in the second ring, and examples of specific actions in the third ring.

- Journal your responses to the following questions: Which faith practices, ministry areas, or actions are most comfortable for you? Which are you drawn to? Which make you the most wary?
- Write down one action you will take in the coming days to practice your faith.

2. Part of Christian living is listening to God's call, day by day, discerning what it is God is calling you—and all of us together—to be and do here and now. Listening and discernment take time. Take a few moments right now to get comfortable and quiet, and then, just listen.

Wrap-up

Be ready to look back over the work your group has done in this session.

Pray

Jesus, be with us on life's paths. Shine your light when we are lost. Walk beside us when we are discouraged. Lift us up when we fall. Strengthen us when we are weak. Through your Spirit, give us peace and hope for the journey. Amen.

SESSION FIVE

faith practices wheel

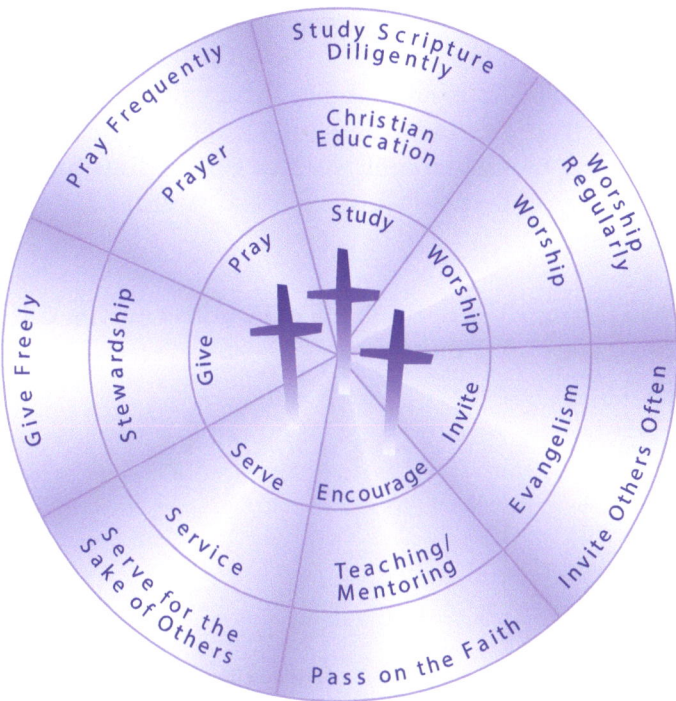

© Evangelical Lutheran Church in America.

Extending the Conversation

Homework

1. Read the next session's Bible text: Hebrews 4:12-13; 5:11—6:12; 10:19-29.

2. Faith is *embodied*. Tomorrow morning when you wake up, stretch your body to increase your flexibility and alertness as you start the day. Take a few moments to be aware of your body. What are your strengths and weaknesses? What are your resources and needs?

3. Choose a sport—basketball, walking, bowling, running, or another. What is the goal of the sport—to make a basket, block a shot, reach a destination, knock over the pins, etc.? Close your eyes and see yourself achieving that goal. Now, set a faith goal for the week—for example, to tell someone about your faith, to give of yourself more freely, to be kinder, to show hospitality. Close your eyes again. Use the sports

Notes

SESSION FIVE

 Notes

image to visualize yourself achieving your faith goal. Use this image throughout the week.

4. Choose one item of instruction from the session Scripture texts. During this week particularly, practice that discipline. Each day journal about the experience—a brief sentence or as much as you want to write. Another option is to list and practice each of the instructions from the texts in rotation, using one each week as a discipline for learning. Think of these as calisthenics to "exercise" your faith.

Enrichment

1. If you want to read through the entire book of Hebrews during this unit, read the following sections this week.
Day 1: Hebrews 11:1-3
Day 2: Hebrews 11:4-40
Day 3: Hebrews 12:1-13
Day 4: Hebrews 12:14-24
Day 5: Hebrews 12:25-29
Day 6: Hebrews 13:1-6
Day 7: Hebrews 13:7-25

2. Prayer, study, worship, invitation, encouragement, service, and giving are important practices of our faith. To support these faith practices, the ELCA provides a variety of materials for individual or group use. Find out more at http://www2.elca.org/christianeducation/discipleship/faithpractices.html.

3. Christians were deeply and centrally involved in the African-American civil rights movement in the 20th century in the United States. Make arrangements to view *Eyes on the Prize,* a documentary series originally televised in 1990 and since then used widely as an educational tool. The series covers the period 1954 to 1985. The title comes from the folk song "Keep Your Eyes on the Prize," a song about faithful perseverance in the face of adversity.

For Further Reading

Bearing the Cross: Martin Luther King, Jr., and the Southern Christian Leadership Conference by David Garrow (New York: Harper Perennial Modern Classics, 2004).

Practicing Our Faith: A Way of Life for a Searching People, ed. Dorothy C. Bass (San Francisco: Jossey-Bass, 1998).

SESSION SIX

Hebrews 4:12-13; 5:11—6:12; 10:19-29

Learner Session Guide

Focus Statement

In Christ Jesus we have the forgiveness of sins—period—no ifs, ands, or buts. When our faith in that promise fails, we lean on Jesus.

Key Verse

Therefore, my friends, since we have confidence to enter the sanctuary by the blood of Jesus, . . . let us approach with a true heart in full assurance of faith. . . . Let us hold fast to the confession of our hope without wavering, for he who has promised is faithful.
Hebrews 10:19, 22a, 23

What If Faith Fails?

 Focus Image

© Design Pics/ SuperStock

Gather

Check-in

Take this time to connect or reconnect with the others in your group. Be ready to share new thoughts or insights about your last session.

Pray

Almighty God, by our baptism into the death and resurrection of your Son Jesus Christ, you turn us from the old life of sin. Grant that we who are reborn to new life in him may live in righteousness and holiness all our days, through your Son, Jesus Christ our Lord. Amen.

Focus Activity

Take a look at the Focus Image for this session. Imagine that the person in the photo is you. What do you see? Whom do you see? Then, change your perspective a bit. Consider this: When God looks at you, what does God see? Whom does God see?

SESSION SIX

 Notes

Open Scripture

Read Hebrews 4:12-13; 5:11—6:12; 10:19-29.

- What words, phrases, or images stood out for you?

- What is your emotional response to these passages?

- What questions do you have?

Join the Conversation

Historical Context

1. At some earlier time, when the original readers of Hebrews were persecuted, they met hardships in joyful faith. Now, in easier times, they seem to have fallen away, neglecting the importance of relying on faith and Jesus Christ.

- Review the session Scripture texts and note signs that the writer is urging readers to return to and rely on faith and Jesus Christ.

2. Having relatively comfortable lives free of persecution can lead to the temptation to neglect faith. Do you agree or disagree with this? Provide reasons or examples to back up your response.

Literary Context

1. The writer of Hebrews uses the educational theory of ancient Greeks, with its different levels of instruction at different levels of educational maturity. Food imagery was a common way of presenting the different levels of maturity.

SESSION SIX

- Read Hebrews 5:11-14 and note the difference between food for infants and food for the mature. What would you describe as "milk" when it comes to basic elements of faith and Scripture? What would you describe as "solid food" for those mature in faith? What "food" is appropriate for children and for young adults?
- Discuss what kind of "food" you would say Hebrews provides to readers.

2. The writer uses an agricultural image or metaphor in Hebrews 6:7-8 to describe God and faith.

- Read Hebrews 6:7-8 and identify the agricultural terms.
- Metaphors rarely have a clean, one-to-one correspondence with what they attempt to describe. As well as you can, explain what the agricultural image tells us about God and faith.

Lutheran Context

1. How is Scripture like a "two-edged sword" (Hebrews 4:12-13)? Some Lutherans understand the two edges to be law (what God asks of us) and gospel (what God does for us).

- Scan Hebrews 4:12-13; 5:11—6:12; and 10:19-29 again. What parts of these texts do you hear as law? What parts do you hear as gospel? How do law and gospel work together here to encourage your faith and point you to Christ?

2. Lutherans emphasize that we are forgiven and saved by God's grace through faith. We rely not on our faith, but on God's faithfulness, shown to us in Christ. The Key Verse for this session puts it this way: "Therefore, my friends, since we have confidence to enter the sanctuary by the blood of Jesus, . . . let us approach with a true heart in full assurance of faith. . . . Let us hold fast to the confession of our hope without wavering, for he who has promised is faithful" (Hebrews 10:19, 22a, 23).

- Role-play a conversation between a sinner and two friends. The two friends have conflicting views on the possibility of forgiveness for the sinner's grievous sin (which shall remain unnamed). One believes the sin is unforgivable, that there is no possibility of repenting and being forgiven. The other friend believes there is nothing outside the bounds of God's grace.
- Describe your reactions to the role-play as the sinner, one of the friends, or an observer.

Notes

SESSION SIX

 Notes

3. Martin Luther taught that the gospel—the good news of Jesus Christ that by God's grace your sins are forgiven—is known by its content. If something doesn't proclaim the gospel, it doesn't matter who wrote it, even if it was the apostle Paul. Likewise, if something does proclaim the gospel, it doesn't matter who wrote it, even if it was Judas or Herod.

- Luther did not believe the letter to the Hebrews should be included in the canon or accepted list of books in the New Testament. Hold a mock debate on this issue. What are the arguments for including Hebrews? What are the arguments against it?
- Tell about a time when the gospel was proclaimed to you by an unexpected person or in an unexpected way.

Devotional Context

1. The promise of forgiveness is God's promise, and God is faithful. When our faith fails, we throw ourselves on God's mercy, knowing that Christ completes our faltering faith. We have not only faith *in* Jesus to sustain us. We have the faith *of* Jesus to rely on when our faith fails. Write a prayer of thanks for God's love, mercy, and faithfulness, and for Jesus the pioneer and perfecter of our faith.

2. In Christ Jesus we have the forgiveness of sins—period—no ifs, ands, or buts. Use the words of confession and forgiveness from the Compline service (*LBW*, p. 155 or *ELW*, p. 321) to give and receive the assurance of forgiveness.

3. If a good friend asked you what you've learned in this study of Hebrews, what would you say? Write down or journal your response.

Wrap-up

Be ready to look back over the work your group has done in this session.

Pray

Pray for one another from Hebrews 13:20-21: "Now may the God of peace, who brought back from the dead our Lord Jesus, the great shepherd of the sheep, by the blood of the eternal covenant, make you complete in everything good so that you may do his will, working among us that which is pleasing in his sight, through Jesus Christ, to whom be the glory forever and ever. Amen."

SESSION SIX

Extending the Conversation

Homework

1. Plan a service of corporate confession and forgiveness with your pastor or worship team. Orders for such a service are included in *LBW* (pp. 293-95) and *ELW* (pp. 238-42).

2. Each evening before you go to sleep, meditate on the words "Jesus Christ is the same yesterday and today and forever" (Hebrews 13:8). Repeat them aloud a few times while you turn out the light.

Enrichment

1. Watch the movie *The Straight Story* (Asymmetrical Productions, 1999), reflecting on perseverance in the journey of faith toward reconciliation.

2. Go online or to the library to learn more about the canon of Scripture—its formation, the controversies about what should or shouldn't be in the Bible, the pros and cons of having a set canon, and what books and texts are not included.

For Further Reading

Stages of Faith: The Psychology of Human Development by James W. Fowler (New York: HarperOne, 1995).

Atonement by Ian McEwan (New York: Anchor, 2002).

Notes

www.ingramcontent.com/pod-product-compliance
Lightning Source LLC
Chambersburg PA
CBHW042142290426
44110CB00002B/87